I Love to Dillydally

Reflections of the Fine Art of Killing Time

Ziad Sawi MD

Contents

How We Kill Time	*6*
Why I Wrote This Book	*7*
The Key to Reclaiming Your Time	*10*
One Thing Leads to Another	*12*
Why You Lack Motivation	*18*
Paying Yourself First Matters	*20*
The Ways We Waste Time	*22*
Want Ninety-One Workdays a Year Back?	*26*
The Most Dangerous Time-Wasters of All	*29*
When You Hear These Lines, Run	*33*
Stay Away from Schedules	*35*
Avoiding Distractions	*36*
Mitigating the Mess	*38*
What to Do When You Need a Mental Break	*40*
A Word about Habits	*43*
Curing Yourself of Dillydally	*46*
Eliminate Busywork	*48*
Let Them Have the Last Word	*51*
Life After Dillydally	*55*
Hypnosis/Guided Meditation Script	*56*

<u>*Reflections on the fine art of killing time.*</u>

The situation was quite familiar: I was so bored that I was flipping through T.V. channels from one to the next, mindlessly scanning the screen as images flashed by. "Nope, nothing to see here…," I thought. Then, I said to myself, "Hmmmm, let's see what's on Netflix. Ah, *Star Trek* reruns. There's something to do. I'll watch that classic episode with a parallel universe." You know, the one with an evil *Enterprise* with an evil Mr. Spock-like beard. Love that episode. Watching T.V. seemed like a waste of time, but since I had nothing else to do, I figured that spending some time with Kirk and company couldn't hurt.

Nothing else to do.

Remember that phrase.

Now, you might be too young to know what *Star Trek* is, much less recall the details of an episode that aired in 1968 (and by the way, if you do have fifty-one minutes to kill, it's worth a look). But whether you are familiar with the Starship Enterprise or not, you have certainly done the same thing, just in a different medium.

How We Kill Time

There are so many options for killing time these days: scrolling down Facebook, endlessly looking at memes, or perhaps clinging to the comments section of an engaging "debate," such as it is, about some topic of truly epic significance and you're about to settle the matter once and for all. Or perhaps you are a blog reader, with your favorite blogs all bookmarked, and you go from one to another looking for a new post to read. Once again, maybe you'll find a new debate in the comments section that you can engage in and settle for all eternity. Or perhaps—and I do not want to name any names here—you spend an inordinate amount of time watching porn … often when you aren't even horny! I don't want to embarrass anyone, but you know who you are. Later on, someone asks you, "What have you done today?" and you think for a moment and struggle to name just one single thing and you can't. So you reply, "Hmmmm, nothing much, really. What did you do?" "Hmmmm, I didn't do much either." Where did your time go? And how can you get it back?

Why I Wrote This Book

This book is not really intended to be a time management book—many books list all the myriad ways in which time disappears from existence. In this book, I will do a little of that. There are also already countless books on the market that offer a million suggestions on how to structure your day and be "productive," whatever that means, in every moment of your existence. And yeah, we will do a little of that too. But the problem that current books don't seem to cover is this: If I asked you what you'd be doing if you weren't watching reruns of your favorite old T.V. programs, if you weren't a social media hound (addict, whatever), if you weren't the captain of the World Wide Web debate society, if you didn't fuck off all day … what would it be?

If it's taking you several moments to answer this question, you have identified the problem. It isn't a lack of time management skills, although time management is a valuable skill to have. No, your problem runs much deeper: it's a lack of motivation and passion. If there really isn't anything you want to accomplish, well, why not watch reruns of T.V. shows that aired long before you were born? I mean, what else are you going to do?

And if your answer is, "I would have done XYZ on Monday and completed some tasks that I am supposed to be doing but am trying to avoid at all costs because I hate doing them," well, there is a problem there too. You are clearly doing something you truly hate and probably shouldn't be doing in the first place. Of course, posting comments on the internet to get the last word in seems like a good idea; anything is better than (insert boring Monday obligations and tasks here). So, the key to time management is not so much to make a list of all the ways you waste time, organize every moment of your life until you are constantly doing something super useful, and build yourself into a superhuman every moment of the day. No, it's something else. Something bigger.

The mechanics of time management are important, and we will touch on them, but our real mission is to find the key to overcoming your dillydally. That key is something that you want, a goal you desire to accomplish, an objective, a passion ... a reason to exist, if you will. If you find that magical "something," then all of a sudden, you will focus; all of a sudden, everything you're doing will lead you a step closer to your goal. In fact, you probably won't need to sit there and plan every moment of your day. Instead, everything will fall into place, as if by magic.

The Key to Reclaiming Your Time

If you don't know where you're going, you will never figure out how to get there. So, if there is no place you want to go, you might as well stay right where you are. Therefore, the first step in reclaiming your time time is not to create a detailed plan on what you will do each and every moment but instead to figure out what you want to accomplish in the first damn place. And it must be something *you* want to achieve and not something someone else wants you to do. That could be anything. Do you want to learn Spanish? Play guitar? Take a trip to Europe? Become fabulously rich? Start a side business for extra cash? It doesn't matter what it is; it just has to be something you actually want and not something you just made up because you figure you should come up with something.

Does nothing come to mind? Don't worry about it. Spend some time thinking about what you want; even think about it while you're doing the things you do to waste time. That really wouldn't be a waste of time; in fact, it might end up being the most productive time you have ever spent. If you happen to come up with a true passion—something that you really want to do or accomplish—then it is worth whatever time you spend getting there.

You cannot get there until you figure it out. So think about it. A lot. For hours. Days. Weeks. Or longer. Don't be in a rush, and don't just think. Talk. To your friends, to strangers that you meet. What kind of work do they do? What are some of the things they have done with their time? What are some things they hope to accomplish? The idea is not to copy whatever they did; the idea is to get an idea. To wait for a spark. When that spark ignites, you'll have your key.

One Thing Leads to Another

Let's say a stranger, someone you might have met in the checkout line at the grocery store, tells you about his trip to Europe, describing the cobblestone streets, medieval towns and castles, beautiful Swiss countryside, golden sunsets in Tuscany, and great museums in Florence. You suddenly develop a passion. You simply must see Europe. But, unfortunately, you are broke. You might as well give up and turn on the porn … or maybe, just maybe, you get motivated. You clear your mind; you make a decision. You are going to Europe, come hell or high water. Now the time management begins, and the fucking-off time ends. Your focus is on getting to Europe because that is *the* most important goal you have at this moment.

The first problem is that travel requires money and you don't have any. So why are you not making money? Job not paying enough? Ask for a raise, if you can. No chance for a raise, and you can't find a better job? Get a second part-time job. Can't find one? Drive for Uber. I do, and I'm a doctor. But that is a story for another book. Stuck at home taking care of kids? Start babysitting for the neighbors. Not enough neighbors? Figure out what you have to do to start a home daycare service and do it. Seriously. If you tell me there is no way to make extra money, you just aren't looking hard enough. And by the way, if you do drive for Uber, don't be shy about telling people your dreams. They might have some of their own, they might have some helpful ideas, and they generally tip better if they think you are motivated to do something.

When you aren't working, you are planning. You are thinking about the cheapest way to get to Europe. Can't think of anything? Google. Or better yet, something like DuckDuckGo or some other alternative search engine—I hate Google. Search for cheap ways to get to Europe. Maybe you qualify for a student flight discount, or maybe you don't. Or maybe you don't even have to fly. Maybe you get there by ocean freighter. That may be a cheaper option. Traveling by sea, you'll have an experience that few others have had, and that's before you even set foot in Europe. You might even be able to work on the freighter and help pay your way there.

Once you're in Europe, won't hotels kill your puny little budget in just three days? Yeah, but that is why God invented Airbnb and a whole bunch of other websites for long-term rentals. There, you can find a room—yes, a room, not an apartment—for as little as $430 a month, which is probably a lot less than what your apartment costs right now. Oh, but you don't know any Spanish? Or German? Or the language of whatever country you plan to visit? Hmmmm, oh well. I guess you go back to porn. Or maybe, just maybe, you realize that learning Spanish will open up more opportunities for you, and you throw yourself into the task. You spend an hour or two every day on Rosetta Stone or your favorite program. Start a conversation with your Spanish neighbors. Listen to Spanish lessons in your car between Uber rides. Notice how all of a sudden, now that you have found a goal, all of your time is used for something useful. Either you are earning money for your trip, learning the cheapest and best ways to get there, or learning a new language. Your dream trip to Europe is about to become a reality.

While you're there, use whatever rudimentary Spanish you've attained to talk to everyone you meet. As a result, your Spanish keeps getting better and better. You keep a travel journal of all the sights you visited and the experiences you had in Spain. You take a million pictures. When you return home, you can't wait to tell everyone about your experience in Spain, so you start a travel blog. You post your pics on Instagram and link to your blog. Once you have five thousand followers, you can earn a little side cash from ads, by the way. Got traffic to your travel blog? You may also be able to advertise there too. Perhaps you will decide to write a book called *My Summer in Spain*, or *How I Lived in Madrid for 25 Cents a Day*, or *How I Earned Money as a Prostitute In Barcelona*. (Side note: I am just joking. I am not recommending prostitution, but then again, I make no judgments.) You publish your book on Kindle. You narrate it and put it on Audible. One thing leads to another, and suddenly, you look back on your accomplishments and wonder how you ever found the time to get so much done.

I am not saying you should stop everything you're doing and head to Spain; I am saying that when you find something you really want to do, all of a sudden, you start making better use of your time. Things come together when you find your passion, step by step.

Maybe in the course of your conversations with strangers, you did not run into someone who told you about a trip to Europe. Rather, this chatty gentleman enthused all about his experiences as a private investigator. You head home and start researching requirements and the nature of the P.I. business and maybe decide it isn't for you, or that you don't qualify for it, or that it isn't worth the effort. But maybe, just maybe, you decide it's the perfect fit. You enroll in some criminal justice courses, or combine it with your existing background in accounting so you can track down fraudsters and embezzlers and various types of financial criminals. You hone your observation skills, learn to notice details, and make a mental note of everything in your surroundings. You start listening carefully to how people talk. Is your intuition telling you they are lying or hiding something? You look around for whatever entry-level position you can get at a P.I. firm and get whatever experience and training you can. Take a martial arts course. Learn how to handle firearms. Do whatever you need to do to qualify for a license. The list goes on. Again, I am not telling you to become a P.I., and I don't know the first thing about a private investigator career (and I'm not just saying that to stay undercover!), but you get the idea. Once you have the goal, the time management falls into place. Otherwise, if there is no place for you to go, you might as well just sit on the couch.

Why You Lack Motivation

Let's talk about the common reasons behind a lack of motivation. We have already gone over the first: your lack of passion. Remember, you simply haven't found what it is you truly want to do. You are stuck in some mundane world of chores and tasks assigned to you by others. It's in those situations when the usual time management books are pretty damn useless. You're organizing every moment of your day so that you can help someone else achieve their goals while you are stuck in mediocrity—that day-to-day purgatory of just getting by. Yes, make sure you type up that report so that your manager can get all the credit and look good. Wash and wax that brand-new Cadillac Escalade so the owner can drive around in style while you walk around in soggy shoes. Rush your passenger to the airport so he can go on his fabulous vacation while you get sent off without a tip. And so it continues, day after day.

If that is your existence, then of course you will do almost anything to escape it. Flip through channels watching nothing of interest. Scroll down Instagram to see what so-and-so had for dinner, because just about anything is better than what you're doing right now. And yet, you reason to yourself, your meaningless work pays the bills, keeps you fed, maybe even pays enough for cable T.V. and an internet connection. Maybe enough for a night out with friends once in a while. A lot of people have it much worse. No job at all. Or they have cancer. Or social problems because of their Tourette's syndrome or Ebola. At least you have your health.

Paying Yourself First Matters

Yeah, it's great to count your blessings, but there's nothing wrong with earning a few more. In the financial world, there is an old adage: pay yourself first. Meaning, no matter what debts you have, no matter what expenses you have to pay, put away some money for you and only you.

This idea holds even more true when it comes to time. Time is the one commodity that can never be replaced, assuming you don't have a time machine. If you lose money, there is always a way to make more, but lost time is gone forever without that time machine. And that is why step one is to first find your real motivation, and step two is to set aside time every single day to work toward making it happen.

How much time? As much as you possibly can. Definitely however much you need in order to plan and execute your escape. There is no point in living with regret, and there is nothing we can do about yesterday except learn from it. So let us take a moment to count all the time we have wasted throughout our lives. Let us then add up all that time and imagine how things would be different if we had applied that time to mastering some skill, getting a part-time job, writing a book, or studying for a degree—a useful one, not one of those 'I graduated from college with a ton of debt and no useful skills' degrees. You don't want one of those.

The Ways We Waste Time

Since I am all about honesty, I will start with myself. But first, let's define what 'waste of time' means. I am going to exclude from this anything you truly enjoy doing, even if it is not really productive. For example, going out with friends, or watching a T.V. program you truly love (*Walking Dead* is not a waste of time, in my honest opinion). And it doesn't count those times when you were so tired, you just had to veg out for a while. Time you enjoyed is not really wasted, even if it didn't bring you closer to some objective. You need that time to keep yourself sane. Instead, our list will focus on that time that gave you no benefit and wasn't even all that much fun. You should always concentrate on cutting that time out first before cutting out all those things that actually keep your mind from exploding.

Based on my experiences, here are some of the top culprits of wasted time. So, here goes:

1. Porn. Guys, you know who you are. You don't have to tell the whole world about it, but you do have to admit it to yourself. Lots of us easily spend ninety minutes or more each day watching porn. Now, maybe if you're super horny, some of that time—let's say twenty minutes—is what we might call necessary for 'energy relief.' That leaves about seventy minutes a day spent stroking away not because you're super horny but because there is nothing better to do. Or at least, there didn't seem to be. Seventy minutes times 365 days equals 25,550 minutes per year. That's 426 hours. Which is 17.5 days—and when I say "day," I mean a full twenty-four hours, not an eight-hour working day. If you are talking an eight-hour workday, that is basically fifty-three workdays a year. What would you accomplish in fifty-three workdays if you truly put your mind to it? At present, those days are consumed with just one thing: porn. And that's not even all your porn time; just most of it. I wouldn't ask you to give all of it up; that's too much. I understand we are mere mortals here, but you could get rid of most of it.

2. Unnecessary time online. That includes social media, checking your favorite blog, and getting into arguments on the internet until you and the other guy are calling each other Hitler, Nazi fascists, communists, etc. What is a reasonable estimate for that time? An hour a day? For many, I bet it is much more. But let's just say one hour. Let's not be too hasty; maybe some of that time is useful. I doubt it, but let's just say it is, or that you just love it so much, you can't let go. So, cut it down from sixty minutes a day to twenty minutes, saving the other forty for something useful. So forty minutes times 365 equals 143 hours a year, which is 10.1 days in a twenty-four-hour day cycle, or 30.4 actual eight-hour workdays.

3. Mindless media consumption. Flipping through 557 channels when nothing's on is one of the biggest time-wasters around. I'm not even sure how much time that is, only that it's a lot. And besides, today it's really not channels; you were probably watching YouTube. Since the internet has taken away so much of our time, it is hard to quantify exactly, but I bet thirty minutes a day is not unreasonable. So let's cut that out. Here I am giving you no slack at all because that is totally wasted time and you need to get rid of all of it. And I'm not talking about all T.V. time—if you absolutely love watching reruns of *Friends* while having dinner, I got you. Don't deny yourself. But when you're in front of the T.V. watching nothing, you have to make a change. I know I had to. Once again, thirty minutes a day times 365 days equals 182.5 hours and 7.6 twenty-four-hour cycles, or almost twenty-three eight-hour workdays per year.

Want Ninety-One Workdays a Year Back?

Broken down into eight-hour workdays, fifty-three workdays could be saved by cutting out just 78 percent of your porn time; 30.4 workdays could be saved by cutting out 66 percent of your wasted internet/social media time; and twenty-three workdays could be saved by cutting out all your flipping-through-channels mindless T.V.-watching time (and that is just the flipping through channels time—I am not asking you to give up all T.V.). Add it all up and you just blew ninety-one workdays a year on absolutely nothing. It was time that was not particularly enjoyable and not in the least bit productive.

Are you beginning to see why your life is fucked up? Why some people have built many empires, and you're living paycheck to paycheck? I once wrote a book called *I Love to Spend*, which is all about wasting money on frivolous things. But while we can always get more money, we will never get the time back, and that's just one year. Multiply those ninety-one days by however many years you have wasted, and now think of what you could have done if you had spent ninety-one days out of each of those years doing something worthwhile. You would be fluent in another language, or two or three. You would be proficient at playing a musical instrument or have earned another $10,400, assuming you're earning just ten dollars an hour. You could have learned a new trade that is more fun or more lucrative than whatever you are doing right now. You could have developed the physique of a Greek god or goddess. But don't be depressed thinking about all the things you could have done. Be inspired thinking about all the things you will do now that you have taken the red pill of time management.

Note that I haven't yet asked you to give up time with friends, your favorite T.V. program, or your favorite hobby. You're only giving up the completely wasted time, and not even all of it. As I stated before, none of this will happen—indeed, none of this should happen—if you haven't found that motivating spark. After all, if you are perfectly satisfied with life the way it is, why change anything? Don't let me or anyone else make you dislike it by coming up with this or that list of everything you are supposedly doing wrong. If you like things the way they are, then you have already found what everyone else is looking for. Sit back and enjoy it. But if you know or feel deep within you that something is missing, it's time to motivate. As I have said and will say again and again, once you find your true passion, all that wasted time will be harnessed and focused on your tasks.

The Most Dangerous Time-Wasters of All

There are things we waste time on other than the three areas we tackled above. In fact, the time-wasters I'm about to discuss now are probably the most dangerous ones as they waste not only your time but your energy as well. They harm your brain space and your emotional wellbeing. I'm talking about anything that is emotionally draining.

This is time spent thinking about bad things. Any bad conversation; any argument where the other person got in the last word; any relationship that sucked away your energy, happiness, or motivation. Anything that impacted your willingness to feel good about yourself. You know exactly what I mean. You replay an unpleasant conversation in your head; think about some unpleasant person who insulted you, offended you, made you angry, or humiliated you in front of others. You revisit it word for word. This individual first robbed you in real life and now robs you of your time, energy, and brainpower, even if he isn't there! You then replay the bad conversation or argument in your mind, this time saying to yourself what you wish you had said at the time. How much time and energy do you waste on such thoughts every single day? How much could you accomplish if those hobgoblins could leave your mind? And even if nothing is accomplished, how much better would you feel if those thoughts didn't plague you? The power of meditation, mindfulness, or self-hypnosis will help you break the cycle.

Then there's the daydreams. These are those thoughts when you imagine yourself as wealthy. Picture yourself as a rock star or an actor or a supermodel. Having a great conversation with a famous person you've never met. If taken to the extreme, this is also a waste of time, but some daydreaming isn't bad. It might motivate you toward getting to where you want to be. At least it doesn't rob you of your self-esteem and energy like negative thoughts do. So spend a little time daydreaming about your favorite thing. Then, take that energy to bring yourself closer to that goal.

Worrying about things beyond your control is another bad habit. This is things like spending vast amounts of time and mental energy thinking about how so-and-so doesn't like you or how you had that fender-bender and are going to have to pay to fix your vehicle. Again, it's time and energy wasted. Another useless dead weight taking up valuable and limited real estate in your brain. Your thoughts are the most precious things. Sure, they seem free, and it doesn't cost you anything to think, but everything you do starts with a thought. So make it a good one.

How much time and energy do you spend thinking about past mistakes and regrets? Time spent thinking about woulda, coulda, shoulda? These are the three most destructive words in the English language, a kind of unholy trinity of despair. Put them out of your head. The only possible positive use of time and energy here is a careful analysis of what went wrong so you can get it right the next time. Other than that, it's a waste. The answer to avoiding this is meditation, self-hypnosis, and mindfulness. The state of the world sucks. I truly hope you are not one of those people who spends hours thinking about the human condition. About world hunger, disease, war, and injustice. I am not saying those things aren't important; they are. Only that thinking about them too much hurts you without helping them. You would be much better off accomplishing a worthwhile goal, or getting rich and donating some money to whatever cause is important to you. Your money will be much more valuable to the people you wish to help and much less valuable to you than your time, mental energy, and precious brain real estate. The peace of mind you purchase with your donation is very precious; it can help you focus your thoughts on some goal you can actually achieve.

Being angry is one of the worst things you can do. I shouldn't even talk about that one. But unless your passion happens to be revenge and how you plan to get it, Edgar Allen Poe-style, which I don't recommend, you should really let go and learn to forgive, or at least forget.

Holidays just suck time away almost by design. How much time do you spend commuting to and from work? That is, assuming you are not one of those lucky ones with a work-from-home job. How much time do you spend waiting in line? Finally, how often do you go to the gym and end up talking to someone you don't particularly like instead of working out?

When You Hear These Lines, Run

Other people tend to place big demands on our time, and one of the ways they do this is through conversation. There are positive conversations, and then there are negatives ones that leave you depleted. How can you tell if a conversation is going to be one of those time-wasters? The following phrases are the most dangerous you will ever hear:

1. "You got a minute?" Well, there are precisely 1,440 minutes in a single day, 480 of which should be spent sleeping, leaving you with about 960 waking minutes. So, surely you can spare one of them. Surely that is easy enough. Until your one minute easily turns into thirty. Do this a few times a day and all of a sudden a huge portion of your 960 waking minutes are gone.

2. "Hey, take a look at this." It turns out to be a Facebook cat video, and there goes another chunk of your time and energy.

3. "Can you do me a small favor?" I am not telling you to be an asshole that never does anything for anyone, but you have to prioritize doing the things you do for yourself first.

By avoiding these types of conversations, you can reclaim some of that time that's otherwise wasted on small talk and useless conversations. Then you can instead spend it on crossing items off your to-do list.

Stay Away from Schedules

Note that I said *your to-do* list, not *your schedule*. Be mindful of your objective, not mindful of the schedule. I am going to advise you to do the opposite of what most time management books tell you: Unless you are an executive in a decent-sized company, do NOT schedule every minute of your day. Instead, assign yourself a task that is part of your long-term goal. So, taking the 'go to Europe and become a travel blogger' example, you may say, "Today I am going to improve my Spanish by going through X number of lessons or reading and understanding X pages of Spanish text or watching a familiar movie dubbed in Spanish and then pausing and repeating each line until I understand everything they are saying." Or if your goal is to become a guitarist, then you could say, "Today I am going to practice this song until I become proficient at it." Or if you are raising money to get to Europe, or saving up to start a small business, you could say, "I am going to raise X number of dollars working at my side hustle job." The idea, and I cannot emphasize this enough, is that when you have the motivation, the time practically saves itself.

Avoiding Distractions

Now, let's talk about distractions. We're living in the age of instant communication. It is great to be in touch with everyone all the time ... unless they are texting you when you're in the middle of your zone. You know, that moment when you are at your most productive, in the groove, moving step by step toward your goal. *Ring-ring* goes your phone. "Hmmm, who could it be? Should I ignore it? What if it's important? I guess I'd better check." Now, before you've even checked, you have lost time thinking about checking. You have lost focus and mental energy that was just a moment ago working hard to bring you to where you want to be.

How do you address this problem? There is no right or wrong answer, as long as you recognize that it is a problem. Some people are easily distracted, easily lose their focus and train of thought, and easily get sidetracked. If that is you, then might I suggest that you let your friends know how busy you are and to text you for severe emergencies only? Otherwise, just turn off your damn phone. If you are the kind of person who smiles, answers a text, and then engages in some back-and-forth repartee that ends with a phone call discussing all the topics you have been texting about, then you need to work with the phone in another room or turn it off.

Are you the kind of person who obsesses that maybe the text you missed is the one that says the house is on fire and you can't concentrate on anything except what text messages you are missing? Well, if no matter how hard you try, you can't let go of those thoughts, then you might as well go ahead and answer the phone or read your text. Read each text you get, but if they aren't about Martian invaders sliding down the chimney and using a ray gun to disintegrate your dog, then don't bother answering and just get back to work. If you absolutely must answer, answer with a single letter: K. You know, the response for those people who are too lazy to write "okay." Perhaps they have read a time management book or two. Whatever your personality, recognize the problem with message distraction and fashion your response accordingly.

Mitigating the Mess

What about a messy workspace? I am a very messy and disorganized person. My workspace is always a mess. It is not because I like it that way. No. Not at all. I love a neat and orderly workspace. I am just too lazy to make it that way myself. Either take the time to clean it up, pay someone else to do the cleaning for you, or take your work elsewhere. Go someplace neat. The library. Barnes and Noble. Whatever. When writing, I like to go to a cheap restaurant and write. It is neater than at home. I like to take a bite of something in between paragraphs. For me, that works great. But it does make me run the risk of running into people I know and a conversation starting up. It is a risk I am willing to take, though, since I cannot work in a messy place, and I am certainly not going to waste my time cleaning up!

Make your own choices. There are many ways to deal with the messy workspace issue. Just a warning, though: do not become a hermit. Hermits are generally not happy and successful people. So, if you meet people you know, politely explain how busy you are, or maybe take a moment to describe your dream and how you are working toward it. My guess is they will understand and go along their merry way. Or if they are people you actually like, and if you have accomplished a lot that day already, maybe sit back and take a break for some good conversation. Good social interaction is essential for happiness and mental health, so enjoy it when it comes along. It is not a waste of time.

What to Do When You Need a Mental Break

Mental breaks are essential. Often, when you're on a roll and accomplishing many great things, your brain runs out of gas. Sometimes, it even starts off out of gas and you can't get anything started—the creative juices just aren't flowing. What should you do? Stare at a blank page or computer screen all day? Vegetate mindlessly? Hint: no. Here are some better ideas.

1. Exercise. No juices at all? Stop and go to the gym or for a jog. The endorphins released during exercise are sure to inspire you and get you in shape at the same time. The juices have been flowing for a while, but now they have stopped? You hit a wall, so do a mini-workout. Stop and give me twenty pushups or sit-ups or squats, or whatever. Again, you'll get endorphins and give your mind a much-needed rest while getting your body in shape.

2. Change gears. Stop and listen to your favorite song. Or listen to an audiobook about how to do exactly what it is you are trying to do.

3. Take a nap. Sleep is never a waste of time. I know many people think of sleep as a waste of time and imagine all the things they could accomplish if they didn't have to sleep, or maybe just sleep an hour or two less. Big mistake. Good sleep is such a great rejuvenator of the mind and body that you should sleep every chance you get. You will thank yourself later. And so, if the juices stop, take a nap. I divide naps into two types: (a) catnaps lasting ten to thirty minutes, which can be quite rejuvenating, and (b) power naps lasting one to two hours. Exhausted after getting home from work? Take a power nap. When you wake up, I bet you will be in a much better position to accomplish things. Your brain feels tired after working on your project for a couple of hours? Catnap. All those cute cat videos and memes might be telling you something after all.

4. Meditate or try self-hypnosis. Perhaps the most powerful techniques of all, meditation and self-hypnosis are such vital tools for mental rejuvenation, positive thinking, self-affirmation, and generation of a true sense of wellbeing that I am amazed so few use them. I like to sleep, which pretty much anyone can do eventually. But meditation is something you get better at with practice. It is always becoming more effective. It will help even the first time you try it, but make it a habit and you will see some serious potential emerge that you never suspected you had. Best of all, it is an inexhaustible tool. Use it as often as you can.

A Word about Habits

There is power in positivity and habit-building. Willpower is a limited force, but habits are self-propagating. That's why diets that depend on an inexhaustible supply of willpower will never work. The fact of the matter is, if you definitely want the donut, sooner or later, you are going to have one, and if you've managed to resist donuts for a long time, chances are that when you succumb, you will end up eating more than just one.

So, should we just give up and stay fat? Well, no. If you are not happy with your health and appearance, let's change it. Instead of saying no more donuts, instead, decide that for each donut you are going to eat, you will first eat at least one cucumber or salad. Then wait a moment and think about how your body feels after that influx of veggies. Most likely, it's energized, refreshed, and your mind is sharp and clear. Your blood is flowing. Your head and fingers are eager to get to work. Your head is racing with new ideas. Your heart is pumping blood with no trouble at all. Your cells are healing and rejuvenating. The vitamins in those veggies are coursing through your body, flowing through your capillaries and entering your cells to do their healing work. The antioxidants are fighting cancer. The silica in the cucumber is making your skin younger and healthier. The lycopene in the tomatoes are powering your libido and sexual energy. Think about all that.

Now go eat that donut. Every last bite. Maybe a second one if you still feel like it. Now think about how you feel. Your stomach doesn't feel quite right. Your brain is cloudy; your liver is struggling to detoxify all the chemicals and preservatives in that donut (or donuts). The spike in blood sugar gives you a feeling of useless, directionless energy, like lifting your foot from the pedal of a Porsche in first gear. Lots of noise with little motion. Now your pancreas, assuming you haven't got diabetes yet, struggles to flood your body with insulin to get that blood sugar under control. Hopefully it succeeds before too much of that blood sugar oxidizes the lipid walls of your cells, causing damage and inflammation, and worsens every condition you have, from osteoporosis in your knees and hips to back and neck pain. Your mind, so crystal-clear and filled with good ideas a while ago, is now just feeling not quite right and probably just wants to lay down and sleep. Your skin, once getting younger and thicker, is now getting oxidized and more wrinkly. The blood sugar is working its black magic on the nerves in your nether regions, reducing erections and penile sensitivity in men, and making women anorgasmic. But on the bright side, that donut was pretty tasty for a moment.

Go through this process every single time you eat healthy veggies or poisonous junk food. Never tell yourself that your iron will is going to stop you from reaching for that honey-glazed. Just think about how you feel before and after each food decision, and let your body be your guide. My guess is, it won't be long before you are eating more and more veggies and fewer and fewer donuts. Maybe not quite zero, but possibly a lot less than you are eating now. The eating of veggies prior to each junk-food binge becomes a habit. The whole entire thought process becomes a habit. The donut becomes a bad habit that gradually is broken.

Curing Yourself of Dillydally

The exact same process can and must be done to cure you of dillydally. Before you dillydally, spend one day using every moment to achieve your goal and think about how you feel. Then dillydally all day and see how you feel. You'll notice a difference right away and act accordingly. Think positively every moment. This means every single thing you do is advancing you toward your goal. The sleep you get is recharging your mind. The food you are eating is keeping your body fit and healthy and young and energized so it can serve you in accomplishing your objectives. The thoughts you think are positive and imaginative, and your mind is busting with energy, new ideas, and creativity. The friends around you are positive people who are encouraging you to pursue your dreams, and your positive nature is in turn motivating and energizing them. Symbiosis is friendship. The fun things you do are giving your mind a much-needed rest so it can focus on the task at hand later. And most importantly, the minutes of the day do not pass until they have called upon you to do something useful with them.

Those periods of meditation are rewiring your neuropathways to enable you to accomplish your goals better and better. They are ridding your mind of doubts and fears and replacing them with confidence and determination. Your positive thinking seeps into everything you do and makes every task and chore easier and lighter and gives you an aura that everyone around you notices without every understanding what it is. They just know they feel better around you and seek your company. All of your thoughts, words, and deeds create brand-new positive habits to enhance your character, and your character will seize your best day. Always keep that progression in mind. Your thoughts are the basis of everything.

Eliminate Busywork

Here's a particularly bad time-waster: busywork. This is probably the second-worst form of time-wasting of all. (The absolute worst is replaying bad events in your head and negative energy.) This is work that, A, does not get you to your goal, and B, does not help you earn a living while you are pursuing your goals. If your day job is unpleasant but is keeping you fed, that is fine until you can find something better—and you should always be on the lookout for something better. At least it is keeping body and soul together. There is no reason to list all the various forms of busywork. Just think back to 50–90 percent of what you did in high school. Or a comparable percentage of what you did in college if it didn't lead you to do something truly better. There was a time when you were forced into those useless tasks, but now, not so much. So don't do them.

Sometimes you are forced to waste time. In that case, the best option is to make the most of these moments. What do you do when you are waiting in a checkout line? Do you stare aimlessly into space? Replay car-crash events in your head? I'd like to suggest some things you could do that would be more productive.

1. Wear a Fitbit. You can record every step you take in the day to motivate you. But if you don't have one, so what? Just start jogging in place. Do that every time you have to wait in line and you will lose a few pounds over a couple of months, look better, and feel healthier—and it didn't even cost you any extra time. Don't waste a moment of time when you don't have to.

2. Not into jogging in place? **Strike up a conversation with whoever is standing next to you.** Go ahead—the worst that will happen is they won't be into it and you will just back off. But you might just have a pleasant exchange and a mini conversation. These actually do make people feel better. You will improve your mood and another person's mood, too. It would be silly not to do it. Plus, every social interaction improves your social skills and conversation skills. This makes you more likable and pleasant. This is especially important if you are the introverted type. Break out of your shell. And FYI, running in place can be a great icebreaker.

3. If I cannot persuade you to be sociable, fine. **Take your headphones with you and listen to something useful.** It's better than nothing.

4. If you forget your headphones, no problem. **Meditate, read, and go through the positive thoughts outlined here.**

Let Them Have the Last Word

We all have a couple of bad habits to break. A big one for many of us is the need to get in the last word. Seriously. The need to win every argument, no matter how trivial, is a massive time-suck and huge waste of mental health energy, both during the argument itself and the subsequent replay of the argument in your head. You know, those times you think about what you would have said at the time if only you had thought of it in the moment. So carefully consider the value of the argument before you go full-bore into it. Of course, if your argument is in a courtroom, by all means, go all out. But if it's a heated discussion on who should be the next president, then perhaps you should just agree to disagree. If it is a marital argument, consider strategic withdrawal from time to time.

Always remember, the best revenge is living well. Spending time and energy dwelling on life's past insults and wrongs done to you serves little purpose. Spending more time plotting your revenge is likely also a waste. You do not have to forgive; you just have to move on. Save the revenge for Edgar Allen Poe.

Enough with the Deal-Hunting

Another time-waster you may recognize from your own life is the habit of spending hours looking for the cheapest deal on something that isn't that expensive to begin with. If you are getting a car, it makes sense. If you are getting a small microwave, not so much. Time has so much value that for small purchases, it's usually more economical to simply spend the money.

Quit Comparing

In addition, many of us spend lots of time comparing ourselves to other people. This is especially problematic if you decide you are second-best and start obsessing about it. Now you suffer the triple whammy of losing time, mental energy, and self-esteem. Comparing yourself to others is fine if that person is a positive inspiration to become better, but it's very negative if you decide it is hopeless and start feeling badly about yourself. The fact of the matter is, as you go through life, you will always encounter people who are better looking than you, smarter than you, have a bigger dick than you or nicer breasts than you. Don't sweat it. You are fine the way you are, and you are going to make yourself even better.

Don't Look Back

Second-guessing your choices and spending hours thinking about how much better everything would be if only you had done X instead of Y is also a poor use of time. Of course, it is hard to stomp out that thinking entirely, and all of us have regrets. So make that regretful thinking positive by making the mistake of X over Y into a valuable lesson you've learned from, and from now commit to doing Y instead of X. Your mistakes are not really wasted if you use them as learning opportunities. Mistakes can be the greatest teachers if you allow them to teach you because we learn the most in life from those experiences that we would avoid if we could.

Make the Most of Your Commute

What do you do when commuting? If you are driving your car and not doing much of anything or listening to music you've listened to a hundred times, maybe you should consider those Spanish language tapes that you can listen to and learn while driving, or an audiobook that you can listen to while driving.

Life After Dillydally

While flipping through channels has its appeal, I have to admit that my life is much richer without watching endless reruns of *Star Trek*. Since discovering the things I'm passionate about, I have managed to reclaim my time and accomplish things I'd never before even dreamed were possible. No longer do I have nothing else to do.

I leave you with this one final thought: Once the motivation comes, it will all seem so simple. Best of luck, because I know you have enormous potential that is just waiting for you to tap it.

To that end I leave you with this guided meditation to help set you on the road to motivation and the best use of your precious time.

Hypnosis/Guided Meditation Script

Sit comfortably in your chair or lie down comfortably in bed. Make sure your back is supported by the back of the chair, cushion, or a pillow. Now that you are in a comfortable posture, I want to bring your hand's palm in front of your face. If you are wearing any glasses please remove them. Your palm should be at least 20 inches away from your face. Support your elbow by putting another hand's palm below it. Now bring your attention to the fingers of the hand facing your face.

Now start to look at your middle finger. Keep looking. The more you look at your middle finger, you will realize that your fingers are spreading apart. Now keep staring at your middle finger. The more you stare at your middle finger the more you will feel your fingers spreading apart. Now you will notice that the more you stare the more your breathing will become gentle and deep. Very deep and gentle. Now slowly you will feel that your eyelids are starting to get heavy and you will have this urge to blink your eyes. Now you will feel your eyelids are getting heavy, heavy, and heavier and you will have this strong urge to blink. Now put your hand down on your lap and blink slowly. Now blink slowly again. Now keep your eyes close and begin breathing very deeply and slowly. Slowly and deeply. Now deeply inhale through the nose and exhale through the mouth slowly. With every breath you take, you will become more deeply relaxed. Deeply relaxed. Now feel this deep relaxation moving upward from your toes to your feet. From your feet to your thighs. From your thighs to your hips. From your hips to your lower belly and from your lower belly to your stomach. Feel the stomach muscles relaxing, deeply relaxing, and this feeling of relaxation moving towards the chest. Feel the entire chest becoming filled with this deep feeling of relaxation. Your breathing will become very deep and gentle. This feeling of relaxation will become deeper and deeper and will move towards your shoulders and neck. Any tension in your shoulders and neck muscles would be released. And then your arms, hand, and fingers will start to relax. This relaxation moves down over your forehead and down over your eyelids and your jaw muscles will relax. Any tension in your muscles of your body will go away. Now as I count from 10 down to zero, your body and mind will start getting deeply relaxed and go into the state of deep deep relaxation.

10..9..8..7..6..5..4..3..2..1. **(Snaps fingers).**

Deep sleep.

Now imagine yourself standing in a beautiful hut covered with magnificent velvety green leaves and smooth long tree branches. Take a deep breath. Now you notice the fine-looking small spiral staircase covered with beautiful tiny white, pink, purple color flowers. A feeling of peace and relaxation will take over you and you will feel a sense of smoothness in your eyes. Now begin walking towards that beautiful spiral staircase covered with beautiful colored flowers to reach a green smooth magnificent looking pathway on the ground below. You notice that this pathway is lined with bright green glorious trees and beautifully trimmed soft grass on the ground. Now slowly step by step come down from this beautiful staircase. Your hand will touch the beautiful colored tiny flowers and leaves warped on the staircase. Take your moment to enjoy the nature around you. Now you have reached the ground and now begin walking on this beautiful splendid green pathway. You will feel the warmth of the sun shining above you from the wonderful white clouds. This warmth of sunshine gives you a sense of protection and you will start smiling. While walking you will feel the soothing softness of grass beneath your feet which will give you a sense of pleasure. While walking you smell roses and jasmine in the air. You will feel yourself getting rejuvenated and energetic. Now you will feel the cool soothing breeze gently wafting around your body as you walk and you will notice how much more you relax and feel refreshed with each step you take. Hearing the birds sing songs from the treetops, you stop a moment to listen to them. Reaching out to lean against a tree, you can feel the rough texture and smell of the bark. Take your moment. A feeling of peace fills you and you will start feeling light, very light, light like a feather A surge of positivity flows through your body and you feel free and happy. Take few moments to let these feelings of liberation and happiness soak you up. Let these feelings rejuvenate you. Your mind and body are ready to respond positively.

You feel free and liberated. You are in control of your life and choices. You are a strong, brave, confident and powerful person who is striving to be a better version of himself/herself every day. You are a doer and proactive person. You are fully in control of your impulses, excuses and actions. You are self-sufficient and has the ability to achieve whatever you set your mind to. You crave growth. You are focused and aware. You believe in yourself to overcome every obstacle. You are driven by your purpose. You accept and respect yourself enough not to procrastinate. You are productive every day. You are disciplined. You are motivated to achieve your goals and make yourself proud. You focus on positive things and radiate positive energy. You choose happiness and positivity every time. Nothing can bother you without your permission. You control how to choose to respond to things. You are unstoppable in achieving what you want.

What a feeling. You are a bold, courageous, motivated, driven, and confident person **(Repeat twice)**. With your increasing confidence and positive aura, you will attract people and opportunities that will add value and positivity to your life. A feeling of peace, confidence and healing fills you up and you start feeling light, light like a feather. A surge of positivity flows through your body and you feel free, happy, calm, and confident more than ever **(Repeat twice).**

Now bring back your attention to this present moment. Take a deep breath. Inhale deeply through your nose and exhale through your mouth. Again inhale deeply and exhale deeply. Now, I am going to count down from ten to one. And as I count ..., you will slowly begin to feel alert, coming back to the present moment and will start opening your eyes slowly. 10...9…8…7…6…5…4…3…2…and 1. Now begin to stretch slowly. Gently and slowly open your eyes, feeling relaxed, positive, peaceful, motivated, confident, and alert.

Printed in Great Britain
by Amazon